OCCUPATIONAL SLAVE

Occupational Slave

From the womb to the tomb, from the cradle to the grave you will be an Occupational Slave Living from Paycheck to Paycheck while Trying to survive on Plantation and Starvation Wages until the day you die!

By Zulu

Foreword

ARE YOU AN OCCUPATIONAL SLAVE? LIVING FROM PAYCHECK TO PAYCHECK. THE ANSWER TO THIS QUESTION IS PROBABLY YES. JOB 14:1 "MAN THAT IS BORN OF A WOMAN IS BUT A FEW DAYS AND FULL OF TROUBLE". THIS IS A TRUE STORY ABOUT A MAN AND HIS TROUBLES OF LIFE STRUGGLES. THIS BOOK IS A BLUE PRINT OF ANSWERS AND HOW TO DEAL WITH THE EVERYDAY PROBLEMS AND THE STRUGGLES THAT LIFE WILL THROW AT YOU. DID YOU KNOW THAT WE ALL ARE SLAVES TO A SYSTEM? YOU DID NOT KNOW THAT DID YOU? THE SYSTEM OF SLAVERY, WHAT IS IT? DID YOU KNOW THAT THIS SYSTEM IS SET UP TO KEEP YOU BROKE AND DEPENDENT ON YOUR JOB. DID YOU KNOW THAT NINETY PERCENT OF THE PEOPLE ARE WORKING FOR THE TEN PERCENT OF THE PEOPLE. WHO ARE THESE TEN PERCENT PEOPLE? PLAYERS OF THE SYSTEM, WHO ARE THEY? ARE THEY BILLIONAIRES AND MILLIONAIRES? WHO IS YOUR MASTER? WHO IS YOUR OVERSEER? WHAT PLANTATION DO YOU WORK FOR? IS IT THE CHURCH? OR IS IT YOUR JOB WHERE YOU WORK?

Occupational Slave is a non-fiction work of art, that the author Zulu lived. He intentionally changed the names of the guilty to protect the innocent. Any resemblance of persons, living or dead is entirely coincidental and fictitiously inspired by the author's imagination. This is from the mind of Zulu.

Cover Design: Terry 'FM' Turner & James Miller Jr

Editor Metrico Vonshay Cohen-Noel

Author: Zulu

Scripture quotation are taken from the Holy Bible, KJV.

Published in the United States by Kindle Direct Publishing (KDP).

ISBN 9781700081858

Foreword Continue

If you want to know the answers to all of these questions in the foreword, you should stop right now and buy this inspiring book Occupational Slave: Living paycheck to paycheck. This book will show you how to break the chains of poverty and hopelessness. How to break free from the chains of bondage on your job. If you want to be free, buy this book and read it from front to back. Do not skip any chapters, because this book was written in perfect order to free your mind. As a man thinks, so is he. Occupational Slave gives you and shows you the answers to your daily troubles. Buy this book and free yourself from the master's hand of bondage. Occupational Slave directs you with explicit instructions on how to break free from the chains of bondage. Once you follow the instructions and apply them into your daily life, you will learn how to become your very own plantation owner and the master of this system of slavery. Did you know that you have a gift to give to the world? If you're tired of robbing Peter to pay Paul, I suggest that you invest a few dollars to purchase this book. Occupational Slave: Living paycheck to paycheck. It's money well invested!

Dedication in Memory of
Professor Dr. Reginald Martin

This book is dedicated to the memory of Dr. Reginald Martin. Professor of the English Literature department of The University of Memphis. Dr. Martin and I became friends in 2005. He taught me the business side of book writing, publishing, marketing and development of subject matter. May he rest in Paradise. For we know that all things work together for good to them that love God, to them who are the called according to his purpose. Romans 8:28

Sincerely,
Your Friend Zulu

CONTENTS

INTRO TO THE PLANTATION

Welcome to Occupational Slave. From the womb to the tomb, from the cradle to the grave you will be an Occupational Slave living from paycheck to paycheck trying to survive on Plantation and Starvation wages. You work hard all your life on a job, or I should say a Plantation. Working hard like a Hebrew slave for minimum wages and you'll never get ahead. Let me explain this (SOS) system of Slavery? eighty percent of the people on this planet will work for twenty percent of the people....ie Billionaires and Millionaires Period. Wait! That has change since I first started to write this book twenty years ago. Now it's ninety percent of the people working for the ten percent of the richest people in the world. Amazon, Microsoft, FedEx, UPS Transportation, YRC Transportation, Kroger, Apple, Penske, Verizon, AT&T, Sprint, Disney, Google, ABC, NBC, CBS, FOX, PBS, BNSF Railway, UP Railway, Norfolk Southern Railway, USPS, CNN, ESPN, Huawei, and any Sports Franchise just to name a few. But the list goes on and on. Do you know who or what's one of the biggest Plantation that does not have to pay Taxes?.......Think about it? Yes, The Church! I will explain later, keep reading. It's hard to make ends meet, when you must rob Peter to pay Paul and here comes Matthew, Mark, Luke, and John with their hands out. Ooh and

don't forget about James he wants some Money too. Hey that's the answer? MONEY? Does this sound familiar to you? If it does Welcome to Occupational Slavery. You are a slave to your job. This is how you know that you're an Occupational Slave?   Liv-

Paycheck to Paycheck? If you miss thirty days of wages and can't maintain your household bills you are an Occupational Slave living from Paycheck to Paycheck. The Federal Government shut down of January twenty-nineteen had eight hundred thousand people crying out for Help. And this shut down affected not only black people but white people, Asian people, all people! For thirty-five days the Government Shut down had these people in dire straits, not knowing when their next paycheck would come. I'm writing this book because I too am a Slave of the system. And if you're in the ten percent guess what? You too are a part of the system because you pay your Taxes to the three people you don't Fuck with......The IRS

P.O.T.S / PLAYERS OF THE SYSTEM

Players of the System (POTS) Who are the Players of this system? These are the billionaires and millionaires and super rich people who doesn't live from paycheck to paycheck because, they got you/us and me working for them, living from paycheck to paycheck. You can't get mad at these people because, this is how the system (Capitalism) works. This is a capitalistic society here in America. This country will never be a socialist society. Why you ask? Because of Money and the lack of money is why you got to have a job to survive in this world. I'll say it now and I will say it again in this book without money you ain't sugar,honey,ice,tea (shit).......lol Now that you know that we all are slaves. I'm going to show you how to become a member of the ten-twenty percent club. Now people can work for you, instead of you working your ass off for them. First things First you must ask yourself how did I become a Slave? The answer is, you was born into slavery when you got your Social Security Number. That's the system that was set up by our forefathers a very long time ago. Have you ever wondered why we pay so many (much) taxes? You buy a house and pay a thirty-year mortgage plus your taxes and insurance. Thirty years later you are a homeowner, right?...... Wrong! Don't pay your taxes and you will find out that you don't own a damn thing! This is the Game (system) that we all are a part of. Without taxes we have no Government of the People. Now you can forget about not paying your taxes. Just ask Wesley Snipes, you don't fuck with the IRS! Now that I. e. you know the truth what can I do about it Zulu you ask? Pay your Taxes on time...... lol. And continue to read this book to learn how to Master this Game (system) of Slavery.

TROUBLES OF LIFE AND THE IRS

"Man, that is born of a woman is of a few days, and full of trouble". Job 14:1

When you're broke, it seems like trouble always come your way. It's always something to keep you spending your money. I said it earlier, you rob Peter to pay Paul and here come the rest of them, Matthew, Mark, Luke and John and don't forget about James he got his hand out too. If you think I'm lying, try to save some money for a trip for you and the family. I'll bet my weeks paycheck that, something will come up, where you need some money. Your car needs four new tires and you don't have the money. What do you do? Where do you get the money? Surely you're not going to steal the money? Maybe you have a money tree growing in your back yard?.......lol And while that is happening, Your hot water tank goes out, Your fridge needs some coolant, the air conditioner stops cooling, the toliet backs up, it's always something when you're broke. God forbid you or your family member gets sick. OMG!..... Does this sounds familar to you? Just think about it? When you're broke, the smallest little things are magnified ten times greater than what it is. It's like someone is watching and waiting on you to try and get out of the hole and, Bam!..... Hits you in the head, Get yo ass back in there! Where the Fuck you think you are going? You're my Slave! I did not tell you, that you could leave the hole. Sometimes I can see why some people take their life into their own hands. But I refuse to give up or give in to the problems or pressure that come my way, because I know that, this is only temporary. I've been poor all my life, and the way I see it, I can't go any lower, so there is only one way up! Philippians 4: 13 *"I can do all things through Christ who strengthens me"*. I don't know if it's satan, or bad luck or it's the cookie monster, but it's always something. And if that's not enough to make you go crazy and lose your mind, here comes the big three people (IRS) saying you owe them some back taxes? What the Hell? I don't owe ya'll Shit! Now you got to spend valuable time trying to convince this government agent that you paid your taxes. And these three people are the only people that I know, that don't have to go to court to sue you. If you owe these people, they can levy your bank accounts, they can seize your property. They can garnish your paycheck. Ain't that a bitch? You're already struggling, trying to make ends meet from paycheck to paycheck. And here come these Mother Fuckers taking your money. You did not go to court and the judge did not make an court order for you to pay these people. These people just took your money. You know that's pimping right? That's Gangster Shit right there! So what ever you do pay your taxes and keep a record of the transaction. Because it's your word against their word. And your word ain't Sugar Honey Ice Tea!

(shit).....This actually happen to me. And who do you think the judge is going to believe Me or the three people of the Government? This is why I'm writing this book to inform you (the public) about my journey of living from paycheck to paycheck. Running from plantation to plantation, just like the slaves of years past. So I advise you too take heed and pay attention. Please Don't laugh, because this could be you one day.......lol.

THE SLAVE TRADE

Working on your job while the overseer is watching you can be troublesome, here's my story: I started working when I was fourteen years old. My mother had to get me a Social Security Number. My first real job and the first time I paid into the Social Security system. My first job was working in the summertime on a lunch truck for the summer job program for the Memphis city school system. It was a good job I had fun working that summer, the job was not hard I was going from park to City Park delivering free lunches. Then my next job let's see I started working at this restaurant I can't remember the name oh I remember orange mound grill the oldest soul food restaurant in the city of Memphis that is own by the same family since nineteen forty-one. From there I went on to graduate high school and then I went on to college and played basketball thinking that I would go professionally but reality sets in and life hits you straight in the face. That's when I said I need to find me a real job. Now I'm working for Memphis packing company a subsidiary of John Morrell meat packing company. On this job is when I first notice this system of slavery. We had a plant manager and three supervisors. We had big nose Iverson the plant manager and the three stooges, Roscoe, Fred and Kenny they were the supervisors. It was like working in Hell on the Kill floor of this plantation. Everybody was bloody and funky by the end of the day. But I enjoyed learning how to slaughter a hog. It was a good job in nineteen eighty-three I was making good money thirteen dollars an hour. I was young I had my own apartment my own car I had so many women I didn't know what to do with them and life was good then we find out that the plant was going to close in nineteen eighty-six. I got to find another job. So, I start looking and I found other little jobs, but they'd never meant anything. That's when God blessed me with a good job. I taught myself how to drive a truck and for the next thirty-five years I have, had a good job working primarily for myself but at the same time I'm still working for the man. You see I was what you call an owner operator. I had my own truck and at one time I had my own authority and the money was coming in here from left and right, life was good, but like all things in life it too came to an end. Now I got to find another job. This time I started working for Memphis scrap metal over there on president island and working for these people Oh my God they had an overseer his name was Jake. I like to call him Jake the snake. And this is how he became the boss. He married the owner's daughter. And the owner felt so sorry for him that he made Jake the (overseer) supervisor. Now Jake comes from poor white trash, and when you give or put someone who never had anything into power, it goes to their ego or I should say their head. They think they are now better than you. I will never forget the day he tried to show us slaves some gratitude and appreciation. He bought everybody some Popeyes chicken and thought he had showed us some humility. You can't buy my respect with a box of chicken! I told him, dam some chicken! You want to show me some gratitude, give me a dollar raise, and I can buy my own dam chicken! I think I pissed him off in front of everybody. And I don't care how he felt. I believe that's when he made up his mind that he had to get rid of this slave? (me). ooh and his wife, the owner's daughter she was so ugly. She had the face of Medusa. She was hideous! Ugly like ugly on an ape! I don't mean to talk about another man's wife, but I have seen a better-looking face on an iodine bottle. Oh my God! Maybe that is why he treated everybody so mean and ugly, because of what he had to go home too? I'm just saying?......lol. This man or should I say boy treated you worse than the Egyptians treated the Hebrew slaves. All my life I have worked for someone and I'm probably going to work for someone until the day I die but I am not going to let anyone talk to me or treat me as though I'm lower than whale shit. I am not your redheaded stepchild. I am not a Hebrew slave, and you are going to treat me like I am a human being, I have a life too. Yes, I work for you. Yes, I get up and go to work every day like a slave for you, but I refuse to let you treat me like I am a Hebrew slave. It's called RESPECT! I don't care who you are or what you are, you should treat people with dignity and respect. So, Jake and I got into it. We had a quarrel over a safety issue, and after a few words it got very nasty he said something, I said something the next thing you know I'm fired.! So, I needed to find another job, Now I started working for M&H construction and these people got an overseer his name was Jose Miguel Gonzalez Jr, they called him junior for short. He was four feet tall and weighed four hundred pounds. He was cross-eyed, had a bald head and he had a speech impairment. (he stuttered). This Mexican Oh My God! This overseer was worse than Jake the Snake. This Mexican was crazy as a road lizard. He treated you worse than these white people treated the Negro slaves, he talked to you so crazy. And I'm not going to let anyone talk to me just any kind of way. I don't care if you're the boss. It's a better way to treat and talk to people. I demand Respect! He told Me that I had to work, and I came to work every day. I did my job, I tried to fit in, but one day I had to take care of some business at the bank and I ask this boss can I take off around three o'clock he said to me, No you cannot take off, and I said, I need to take care of something at the bank. And he said, if you take off find another job. And I said. What! Find another job? What do you mean? He said I hired you to work and I need you to work no questions asked! And I said, Boss we have been working for twelve hours a day for seven straight days. I have not had the chance to go to the bank. Or do anything I haven't had a chance to cut my yard and he said that's not my problem. What? Yeah, it's my problem, I am not your slave and I'm going to the bank. And he said, if you leave work, find another job. And guess what? That's what I did, I found another job, or I should say, I found Love. Let me explain. In January of the year twenty sixteen I started to work at this new Plantation. I will never forget my interview with my new boss Jeff Johnson. He was as cool as a cucumber, very smooth. But I must give myself some credit too, because I was as cool as the other side of the pillow. Because I needed this job. I needed their Insurance and all their benefits.

This Plantation makes all the other Plantations look like a welfare case. I'm talking about The Kroger Plantation. And for the first time in my life, I'm happy working for this Plantation. Wait a minute, I don't come to work, I come to Love every day. When I was a little boy, my father said to me (boy try to find something you Love to do to make a living at) and I said, Why pops? He said, (If you find something you Love to do to make money, you will never work a day in your life). I did not know what my Pops (Father) was talking about at the time. Now that I'm a grown man I understand exactly what he was trying to teach me. I drive trucks for a living, and I love it. I love it so much, that I have been driving since nineteen eighty-six. When I'm driving, It's only Me, Myself and I and God in that truck. I love the peace and quiet that come with driving. I can stop whenever I want to get something to eat and the boss is not looking over my shoulders. I can talk on the cell phone and don't have to worry about the boss saying get off the phone. As a matter of fact, I'm the boss while I'm driving to my destination. I love my Job so much that I have written a book about it. Cross Country (From behind the wheel of an Eighteen-Wheeler from The Black Perspective). Now back to this book……

The overseers here at Kroger treat you with Respect and dignity. They treat you like you're their Family, because you are a part of their Family. The Kroger Family of Stores. We are all part of a chain of associates who make Kroger as strong as the weakest link in the chain of associates. In other words, I got your back, you've got my back. And that's the way it should be. Now there are some employees (slaves) who say that Kroger ain't shit! That Kroger don't pay enough money. And the bosses don't give a damn! This might or might not be true? I do know that the Kroger Plantation is no different than any other plantation. If you think I'm lying just fall dead and see what happens? It's the next slave up-!...........lol. And here's proof that it doesn't matter who you are, your job can be terminated at any time. The number two man at the Kroger plantation, Carlos was escorted to the parking lot, followed by two supervisors Derek and Jim. yes, they were fired! I don't know why or what happen, but it just goes to show you that the master doesn't give a dam about you. All they care about is the bottom line, which is how to make more money. That's why it's good to have a union. I will tell you later about the union. But all I can speak on is how they have treated me. I Love this job (Plantation) so much that I'm going to retire from here when the time comes.

THE OVERSEER

YOUR MANAGER, SUPERVISOR OR BOSS?

If you take a closer look at this system that has been put in place you will find that it's all the same. There's a slogan that says the more things change the more they remained the same. Occupational Slave is no different than the slavery of time passed. Will you admit that we all can't be the chief we got to have some Cowboys and Indians everybody can't be the chief e.g. the master , the boss, the supervisor, the manager somebody has got to do the hard work and have you ever notice that the People who work the hardest are the People who make the least amount of money and the people with the degrees don't work hard but make a huge amount of money. So, if I was you, I would get my education and earn my degree it pays off in the long run. Time will be on your side, but you got to give credit where credit is due these white People who set up this system was smart. Smart how you ask? Everybody is a slave now, not just black People or Mexicans, or Latino's. White People are slaves now, Yes, I said, White People are a part of this system of slavery (S.O.S) because you got to pay your taxes and pay your bills. Just like the rest of us that's why I know that socialism will never work here in the United States of America this is a capitalistic society. The powers to be or the master's of this system don't discriminate aginst race, color, creed, national origin, sex, young or old. If you got a strong backbone, yo ass can get up and go to work on the plantation. These overseers that operate these plantation are some of the rudest, obnoxious, arrogant assholes that I have ever seen. They don't give a dam about the employee (slave), and that's why so many slaves (employees) snap when they get fired, because of how they have been treated up until that point. The people in this world today has changed so much, that you can't talk or treat them any kind of way, like how the masters used too. Back in the days when people allowed the overseer to get away with murder, you could say anything to the slave. Now-a-days the slave is coming back to the plantation with death on his mind. He's sick and tired of the bullshit that his boss (the overseer) is doing to him. You think about it? People who have been working on the plantation for five, ten or twenty years, and they have got a mortage and other bills, and the big bad boss (the overseer) says you're fired! Some people snap and lose all control, thinking that life is over. Go get a gun and you know what happens next? So I'm writing this book in hopes that it might help someone, to think before they act. It's not the end of the world. There are other plantation with better benefits and better people. I know how it feels, when you get fired from your job, that you have given your heart and soul too. You're hurting inside and it seems that nobody gives a dam about your feelings. Then you get home to tell the wife.

OMG! I will never forget what my wife said and did that day when I got fired from the scrap metal junk yard. She acted like a dam fool that day. She was hollering and cussing and fussing. I guess she thought that the world had come to the end? You see a woman likes money, and I guess she thought that I was not going to make any more money. I think that's why she blew a fuse that day. But like always I found a better plantation (job) to work for. I knew that I would bounce back on my feet, because I have been fired so many times from so many different plantations that I could write a book about it..........lol.

MONEY...

ave you ever heard this slogan "if it doesn't make money it doesn't make since"? it's all about the big head hundred-dollar bill it's all about money! First Timothy 6 and 10 says "for the love of money is a/ the root of all kinds of evil, for which some have strayed from the faith and their greediness and pierced themselves through with many sorrows". I say for the lack of money is the root of evil. I don't want to preach to you, but that scripture means don't be or get greedy when it comes to money. You see money in itself is not an evil thing but for the love of money and the lack of money is when the sin begins so don't be greedy, but I got to say this, without money you ain't sugar, honey, ice tea (shit). I don't know of any woman who wants a broke ass man, when you got money People treat you with respect. Yes, Sir Mister Zulu no Sir Mister Zulu when you got money everybody wants to be your friend. Now this is a contradiction to what the church teaches. But wait a minute did you know that the church is one of the biggest plantations and they don't have to pay taxes. So ask yourself, is money the answer to my problems? I'm going to give you the answer in a later chapter call problems with money.

THE UNCLE TOM SLAVE

THE SNITCH ON THE JOB

Let's talk about the uncle Tom slave you know the house slave, the slave that love to kiss the master's Ass. You know who I'm talking about every plantation has one. Back in the days of slavery they were called house niggers. Yes, boys, ass kisser, I.e. Uncle Toms. They tell everything they see to the master. But they never tell what they do. On your job (plantation) you have some-body who is an uncle Tom. Begging, hoping and looking to get some special points with the overseers, (The Boss, Supervisor, Manager). Now-a-days you got so many Uncle Tom ass kissing slaves it doesn't make any since, because kissing ass don't get you nowhere now-a-days. I see so many ass kissing uncle toms on this

Job (plantation) here at Kroger it's a damn shame. Ooh I didn't tell you about my new plantation (job) I'm working at Penske part-time. Yes, you need two jobs or maybe three to survive these days. Back to the story, I can't stand uncle tom ass kisser. They get on my last nerve. I have a saying, (if you're going to kiss somebody's ass make sure that ass is taller than you). I'll be damn if I'm going to stoop down and kiss somebody's ass that's shorter than me. I'm not going to do it! I don't kiss ass. I don't smile and grin all up in the master's face. Trying to get some special treatment. Some People love it to death. Me I just don't kiss ass. All I want is my paycheck for what I have worked for. I don't need to be all up in the master's face. I came to this plantation to make a paycheck not to make a friend, not to make a buddy. A paycheck. And it's the same dam thing over here at the Penske plantation. These slaves trying to get special treatment. I'm not going to name any names, but they know who they are? This one salesman who we shall name/call him Roy, has a little position with the Penske plantation and this asshole thinks he is the big bad boss, He thinks he is the (HPIC)

Head Person In Charge, when he's only a plantation overseer and his job can be terminated at any time. Let me try and give you a vision of this person. He's young and dumb and full of ambition. He's very emotional and self-conceited. He tries to look like he's educated, but he's only a nerd, like the nerds from the movie revenge of the nerds. He looks and talks like a college geek, that thinks that he knows every dam thing. You can't tell him shit! He doesn't listen very well, because he thinks he knows it all! My father trained me to always be aware of a person who thinks that they know everything! Roy, he reminds me of the President of the United States of America (DJT 45) who knows more than his Generals? Watch out for people like this, they can be dangerous to your health! My father taught me, that if you want to know something about a person. Just shut up and listen. People will tell you everything about themselves, if you would close your mouth and let them talk. That's what I do when I first meet people. Especially when I start to work at a new plantation. On my first day on this plantation I notice that Roy had to have the last word in the conversation. He always overruled the other people who was giving their opinions about the subject of the conversation. So one day this dam fool, he said that I was sleeping on the job. This dam fool tried to get me fired. Let me give you some details on what happen. I'm what they call a hiker? I drive the Penske bob trucks and tractor and trailers from dealerships to dealerships and to Home depot's customers. So, one day I'm in a sleeper truck writing on this very book when this son of a bitch come looking for me knocking on the truck. I just let the dam fool knock. That's when he calls somebody up the chain of command and tells them that I'm asleep in the truck. If I wanted to go to sleep, you better believe that I would not have parked on Penske's parking lot. But this mother fucker.... Oh My God! If you ever want to see a true ass kisser come to Penske. He wants to be the big bad boss so bad that he doesn't just kiss's ass he chews on people asses. You see I watch people very close. Remember my father taught me that if you want to learn or know something about a person shut your mouth. Shut up! And listen, they will tell you who they are in about ten minutes. When I started working here at the Penske plantation I just sat back and listen to all these people and how they were trying to impress each other. And I saw that this salesman likes to give orders, he wanted his voice to be heard. He wants to be the (HPIC). Head Person In Charge! The Boss! And this is the snitch on the Penske plantation. Every plantation has an asshole. It's all the same at any plantation, that's why you should try and find a good plantation with good benefits and stay there until you can retire with a good pension. And always remember that, every plantation has an uncle tom slave who is the snitch on the job!

THE LAZY SLAVE

THE ALWAYS LATE WORKER

Now let's talk about the lazy slave you know the slave who wants a big paycheck but have not done a damn thing to earn a big paycheck. The lazy slave just rides the time Clock and be up in the master face like he or she is working they ass off. The lazy slave wants something for nothing always skinning and grinning trying to scam the next slave. There is a saying, one rotten Apple will spoil the whole barrel. One lazy slave can influence all the other slaves to be lazy. The lazy slave is always late or just in time to make roll call or punch in on the Clock. I don't like lazy People. I believe that lazy people are the reason why so many plantation owners be so hard on all the other slaves/workers, because they think that everybody is lazy? But this is so far from the truth. I believe that the lazy slaves are the ones who steal from the owners. The lazy slaves are like buzzards and vultures, always waiting on someone to give them something? Let me explain it this way. People are like three birds? You have a Hawk, an Eagle, and the lazy buzzard or vulture. The hawk is a proud bird who catches his food. If he doesn't catch his food, he doesn't eat. Some people are just like the hawk, if they don't get up and go to work, they don't eat. They will never take charity or a handout. Some people are just like the hawk? Hard working and never looking for the government to give them something. Now the eagle he too is a proud bird, if he doesn't catch his food he doesn't eat, but did you know that the bald eagle, the American symbol, once he finds his mate they mate for life? Yes, for life! I'm like the bald eagle, I get up every day and go to these plantations so that I can make some money to be able to take care of my family. I'm married for life to my wife, until death do us a part. I'm proud just like the bald eagle. Now let's talk about the lazy, good for nothing buzzard or vulture. Did you know that a buzzard or vulture will sit in a tree, in the wilderness starving to death, see a rabbit or squirrel and will not try to catch it, just sit there waiting on it to die? How lazy can you be? Some people are just like the buzzard or vulture. Waiting on someone to give them something for free. Too dam lazy to get up and go to work. Sitting around watching the hawk and the bald eagle get up and go to work, then come to their nest/house, kick the door in and steal what they have worked for. Now answer this question which bird are you? The Hawk, The Eagle or the lazy Buzzard? I can't stand lazy good for nothing people. There is nothing in this world that is free? Look at the word freedom. If you think that it's free, you're dumb! FREEDOM! They (POTS) tell you it's free to get you there to sell you something? My father warned me about things that are supposed to be free. Remember this is a capitalistic society. It's about making money. If it doesn't make money, it doesn't make since! This is what the Bible says about lazy People. Proverbs 10:4-5 "he who has a slack hand becomes poor, But the hand of the diligent makes rich. He who gathers in summer is a wise son; he who sleeps in harvest is a son who causes Shame. Proverbs 14: 23 "in all labor there is profit, but idle chatter leads only to poverty". Proverbs 19:15 Laziness cast one into a deep sleep, and an idle person will suffer hunger. 1st Timothy 5:8 "but if anyone does not provide for his own, and especially for those of his household who has denied the faith and is worse than an unbeliever. In other words that lazy good for nothing slaves will never have anything to show for his labor or work because he or she is lazy, so this book is not for a lazy person (slave). As a matter of fact, the lazy slave won't read or buy this book. And that's a damn shame! Let's move on to the next chapter.

SYSTEM OF SLAVERY

S.O.S

What in the world are you talking about Zulu? System of Slavery! (S.O.S). There is a system that has been program into our psyche. It has been programed deep into our souls and minds that it has become institutionalized and established as a social event in our daily lives. This system is designed to keep you broke and dependent on your job (Plantation). What are you talking about Zulu? Keep reading, I'm going to explain. Have you ever noticed that every month there is a holiday or President Day or some special day to get you to spend your money? Check this out! Please see chart on the back pages of this book because it's too many to name them all. For the sake of this book, I'm going to name the major events, or I should say holidays to get you to spend your money every month.

* * *

January- First day of the. New Year. Happy New Year. MLK Birthday, Washington's Birthday.

* * *

February- Happy Valentine's Day. And let me say this about this Love day. If this is the only day you think of/about and show the one you Love that you appreciate them, well shame on you. I think about the one I love twenty-four seven and three hundred sixty-five days a year! Now smoke on that! Back to the book.

* * *

March- St. Patrick Day.

* * *

April- Easter. And let me say this about this day. What in the world is a rabbit and some eggs got to do with the Life, Death and Resurrection of our Lord and Savior Jesus Christ? Absolutely Nothing! And Easter is a big money day for the church, because people who never go to church come to church on this day, to give their tides and offerings. The men buy a new suit and show up at the local church, looking for a blessing. I do believe that they think that this will help them into the kingdom to come, but I got news for them. You can't buy your way into the kingdom. If that was true, all rich people would go to heaven. (Jesus said it's hard for a rich man to enter heaven, it's like a camel trying to go through the eye of a needle). But this Easter Sunday, this is a clever way to get you to spend your hard earn money.

❊ ❊ ❊

May- Memorial Day, Mother's Day.

❊ ❊ ❊

June- Father's Day.

❊ ❊ ❊

July- Happy 4th of July.

* * *

August- you get a break.........lol.

* * *

September- Labor Day.

* * *

October- Halloween. And this day is almost as big as that day in December?

* * *

November-Thanksgiving Day.

* * *

December -Now the biggest money day of them all! Merry Christmas. This is supposed to be Jesus Christ's birthday. This is the biggest lie ever told. Jesus Christ was not born on the 25th of December! But you have been told this for so long you now accept this to be fact, when it's fiction. There are four things you should know about the truth. 1.The truth can hurt you.2. The truth can change you. 3. The truth can set you free. And 4. The truth can get you killed. Please don't kill the messenger! I'm only telling you the truth. The very Bible you read says: The Truth shall set you Free! Now that your eyes have been opened and you now know the truth, what should you do? So, all year the System got you spending your money on things you probably don't need in order to keep you broke and dependent on your job, therefore you are an Occupational Slave working on somebody's plantation. Don't get mad, get even! I'm going to show you how to get even.

THE GIFT

THAT'S IN YOU?

The Bible says in 1ˢᵗ Timothy 4:14 "Neglect not the gifts that's been given you". There are seven spiritual gifts of the Holy Spirit. Wisdom, Understanding, Counsel, Fortitude, Knowledge, Piety, and the fear of the Lord. 1ˢᵗ Timothy 4:14-16 "Do not neglect the gift that is in you, which was given to you by prophecy with the laying of the hands of the eldership. Meditate on these things; give yourself entirely to them, that your progress may be evident to all. Take heed to yourself and to the doctrine. Continue in them, for in doing this you will save both yourself and those who hear you". In other words, everybody has a gift or talent that only God gave you. Use it before you lose it! What I'm trying to tell you is step out on faith and start your own plantation (business). You have a gift or talent that is in you. Some people can play the piano and never had a lesson. Some people can repair small engines and cars and they never went to mechanic school. Some people can sing, I should say sang and never had voice lessons. Some people can cook and never read a cookbook or took a class on cooking. Everybody has a gift or talent so use it to your advantage. Don't be afraid of failure. One of the secrets of life is trying to figure out why are you here? Another secret is what is my gift or talent that God gave me to give to the world? Once you figure out what your gift or talent is start a business (plantation) or use it to make money. Don't be afraid of failure! Failure is when you don't try. You just give up. Just because your business went out of business don't mean that it was not a good idea. It might have been the wrong location or the wrong product. I have stepped out on faith so many times, I can't count them all. You see I will never give up! Until I'm dead and buried in the grave. I'm always thinking about how to make some money with my mind. One of these ole days I'm going to be successful in my quest to have my very own plantation. And then ninety percent of the people will be working for me. You too can achieve this American dream. Set your goals and aim high, because the sky is the limit.

SHARECROPPERS...

OWNER OPERATORS

ow I want to talk about Sharecroppers. These are the people I call Owner Operators and Sub-Contractors. When the federal government had the shut down in January twenty nineteen not only did eight hundred thousand gov't workers was living from paycheck to paycheck, so was the two million sub-contractors who I call sharecroppers was living from paycheck to paycheck. I was an owner operator back in the day. I had my own eighteen- wheeler truck and I thought I was doing good in life. I was leased on to a good company, so I thought I was going to get rich. I got it made right! Wrong! The system is not set up for you to get rich working for somebody else's plantation. Remember ninety percent of the people are working for the ten percent of the people. But there are very rare occasions when the slave turned the table on the master. Case in point, rumor has it that Ervin (Magic) Johnson point guard for the Los Angeles Lakers. After twenty years of service walked into the office of Dr. Jerry Buss the owner of the Lakers and asked him if he wanted to sell the Lakers? I sure wish I could have been a fly on the wall, to see the look on Dr. Buss's face. How can this slave who I have employed for twenty years walk into my office and offer to buy me out? Right after that magic has the AIDS virus or HIV and that was the last you heard of magic. They had to slow magic down. Who is they? *The Players of the System (POTS).* Here is another high-profile person. Bill Cosby, rumor has it that when the Cosby show was number one. Bill Cosby walked into NBC and asked to buy NBC. Soon after that the show was canceled! They, the (*POTS*) will never allow this to happen. That's like the slaves of years past trying to buy the plantation. That's unheard of, the slave buying the plantation

THE SPORTS PLANTATION

THE FRANCHISE

If you would really look at the three major sports you will find that they are the closest thing to a real slave auction, like they used to have back in the days of slavery. take football for instance, i have never been to a live auction of human flesh, but a football combine comes mighty dam close. at the combine you have coaches and executive and trainers measuring and testing these players with practically no clothes on just like back in the day at an auction. they the slave owners would strip you naked and sell you to the highest bidder. if you would take a closer look you will see that a football combine is no different than an auction. they (the *coaches and owners*) test how fast you can run in forty yards, how high you can jump, how much weight you can lift. They check your wingspan from fingertip to fingertip, how big are your triceps, biceps, calf's and your hamstrings. Hell, they even check your urine.........lol. And yes, the billionaire owner is going to make you a millionaire player and he owns the rights to you when you sign that multi-million-dollar contract. In other words, he owns your ass! Lot, Stock, and Barrell! This is the system of Professional Sports Franchise. Remember the NFL strike or lockout of twenty eleven. Billionaires and Millionaires arguing over a thirty- billion-dollar pie. The players union wanted more money and the owners did not want to pay the price of luxury for the players. That's why I don't spend my hard earn money on professional sports anymore. Why you ask? When it

was all over said and done guess who paid the price? You guess it? Me, you, us the fans. The price of season tickets went up. The food at the stadium went thru the roof. A cup of beer is ten dollars. The owners slowly and maliciously raised the price of everything so they could pay the players union. If you think I'm lying, just try to attend a super bowl. The nose-bleed seats are two thousand dollars. A poor man like me can't afford to take his wife and kids to see a super bowl game. The NFL is a huge plantation with thirty-two masters sitting at the very top making decision about a player's life. And I don't mean to pick on the NFL, but the NBA is no different. It's a plantation also! Major League Baseball same thing, A huge plantation. Now of course these players don't live from paycheck to paycheck, but they do pay their taxes and most players leave the game broke. Why? Because most players don't know how to invest their money. No one gave them advice, on how to prepare for retirement. If you have a pile of money and you are pulling money from that pile and you never put money back into the pile, what's going to happen to your pile? It will disappear. You take the average player give him a huge contract and in six years the money is gone. Because he's always spending and not saving. He has no supplemental income. No money coming into the pile. Case in point Terrell Owens they say he's broke. I don't think so?.......lol. in the NBA just ask Antione Walker he signed a grantee ninety million dollars contract in 1989-90 and today he is dead broke. The system is designed to keep you broke and depending on your job. When you're rich the system is always trying to get you to spend your money. Everybody is your friend.

People will give you things on credit, just to get your business. The snakes and vultures come out of nowhere to get your money! So be careful, all you future ballers, be wise and invest your money. The System of Slavery is waiting on you to slip up and fall for the hype of the game.

EVOLUTION OF THE GAME......

The game has change, because of morden technology. We are living in a time of history that mankind has never seen before. We have the world wide web. People call it the internet. It used to be that you would walk into a plantation (business building) and fill out an paper application to apply for a position to work at a plantation. Because of technology and the internet, you don't have to leave your living room couch. It's amazing how the *Evolution of the Game* has changed the way the plantations are being operated these days. If you want a job working on any plantation, you have to go online and apply for the position, then give them your e-mail address and they will do a background check to see if you're a criminal. If everything checks out okay, they the human resource department will contact you by e-mail and set up an appointment for a live interview. This is when you would go to the plantation and actually meet someone that works for the plantation. At this meeting, the boss or supervisor are trying to size you up, to see if you're what they are looking for as an employee (slave). They are trying to see if you're crazy? You know your mental state of mind? Everything has change, the time clock now-a-days don't use paper anymore. Today they use your finger print or facial recognition technology. I wonder what they will invent in the future?

CAPITALISM

Webster's dictionary define Capitalism as an economic and political system in which a country's trade and industry are controlled by private owners for profit, rather than by the state or federal government. Capitalism is an economic system based on the private ownership of the means of production and their operation for profit. Characteristics central to capitalism include private property, capital accumulation, wage labor, voluntary exchange, a price system, and competitive markets. There are benefits and drawbacks to a capitalist economy. The broad purpose of capitalism is to prescribe how individuals will participate in creating their own wellbeing. At a practical level it gives us at least three institution. Markets: to exchange our capital, Money: to transact our exchange and a legal system: to protect our rights of ownership. Is the United States of America a Capitalist Country? Yes, I think/know so!.......lol This is what the Brookings Institution said on March 11, 2009. Even if Barack Obama's proposals were adopted, the United States would remain a capitalist country. Let's be clear what we mean. Roughly speaking, cap-

italism implies that markets and market transactions are the principal drivers of economic activity. Put simply, a capitalist system is controlled by market forces, while a communist system is controlled by the government. Who invented Capitalism? The originators of classical political economy. Adam Smith, David Ricardo, James Steuart and others created a discourse that explained the logic, the origin, and in many respects, the essential rightness of capitalism. Capitalism is more moral. The capitalist believes that people can make their own best decisions. This is the basis of the free market with millions of people making individual choices. Statists believe the common man is incapable of making good choices, so an elite must intervene and make choices for the people. So, there you have it in a nutshell. We are all slaves to this system of Capitalism. I'm glad you have read my book up until this point. Here are some other books I think you should read to help you understand this book better. The Principles of Ray Dalio. He is a billionaire and founder of Bridgewater Investment Group. Shut up and Listen by Houston Rockets owner billionaire Tilman J Fertitta. The other book Managing your Money with God as your Partner. Publisher Freeman-Smith LLC. If you want to know or see what pure capitalism is, just look at the Dallas Cowboys Football Franchise. The owner Jerry Jones bought the franchise in 1989 for one hundred forty million dollars. Today in the year of twenty-twenty forbs estimate that the franchise is worth five billion dollars. That's Capitalism at its finest! Remember if it doesn't make money? It doesn't make since.

THE MASTER

THE OWNER OF THE PLANTATION

This is the (HPIC) Head Person in Charge. The person who pays or signs your paycheck. The Boss or the owner of the plantation. Roger Penske started this plantation (business) with a few hundred dollars, and now forty years later it's worth three billion dollars. Jerry Jones owner of the Dallas Cowboys is one of thousands of masters who are billionaires. These billionaires and millionaires belong to an elite social club. They don't work like you or me on a nine to five job.

They own the plantation where you and I must work to maintain a living, this is the system of capitalism at it's finest. Now the trick to owning the plantation is to keep your employee (slave) broke and dependent of his or her job. The bible speaks about how the masters should treat his servant and how the servants should obey their masters. I know that some people will not want to recognize my theory about this book that I call occupational slave. I can hear them now, I'm not a slave, I'm an employee. Some will even say that they don't live from paycheck to paycheck. There are millions of people who are in denial and will never accept the cold hard facts, that they are suffering on a daily basics. If you would tell the truth and shame the devil, you would see that there are some and maybe a lot of masters (the boss) on your plantation (your job) who don't give a dam about you or your family. All they care about is the bottom line. Are you making them money? Remember if it doesn't make money, it don't make since! That slogan is the golden rule of business 101. That's why I'm going to try and change how the master treats his slaves (employees). I pray that one day I start my own plantation (business) and I'm going to give my slaves (employees) RESPECT, because that's all I'm asking for in return is RESPECT, and do your job. You see I know how to treat people with dignity and respect. All I'm asking for is people to be responsible for their actions. If you need to be off say so. We all have a life beyond this plantation (job) so be a man or woman about it. We are all grown folks, so act like it. I don't believe in stealing. Ask for what you want? If I catch you stealing, That's It! You're fired! If you need some money just ask? You don't have to steal it. Don't lie, because you don't have to. Tell the truth and shame the devil! I'd rather deal with the truth and be hurt than to be happy with a lie, because one day the truth is going to come out, then people will lose all trust in you. Trust is like an egg, once it's broken you can't put it back together. so start out on the right path, and you can never go wrong.

THE CHURCH...

Let me say this straight out of the gate. This is going too piss off a whole lot of preachers and church folks, but I don't care if this offend them. I will not tell a lie, because God hates a liar. Read your bible so that no man can deceive you. Matthew 24: 4 (and Jesus answered and said unto them, *take heed that no man deceives you. For many shall come in my name, saying, I am Christ; and shall deceive many.* Now I could write a book about the church and maybe one day I will. But for right now I'm writing about how the church and people are taking advantage of the tax loophole. I know that I'm going to make some enemies in the church, because they (the preachers) don't want you (the members) to know what's going on behind closed doors. And let me say this, not all churches or people are taking advantage of the system. I'm not suggestion to anyone to stop giving or going to church. If you are a member of a church, God bless you! But did you know that you can find Jesus anywhere all by yourself? (1Corinthians 11:3 *But I would have you know, that the head of every man is Christ; and the head of the woman is the man; and the head of Christ is God).* What this verse means is? In my house God is the head of my Life, then Christ Jesus is my savior and I the man is the head of my wife. Also, Jesus said in Matthew 18:20 (For where two or three are gathered together in my name, there am I in the midst of them). There is nowhere in the bible where Jesus said build this building and the sinner will come. What I'm about to write about is how the religious organizations or I should say these people take advantage of this system of Slavery. A religious institution does not have to pay taxes. The founding fathers made sure that The Church is tax-free from the Government. Separation from church and state means no taxes, right? So why is this phrase on money and in every courthouse and Government building (In God We Trust).

The Church ask you for your tides and offerings which you can give and get a tax write-off for giving to the church. This is a slick way of deceiving the Man, or I should say the Government. You know the System. If you're rich this is a tax write-off. Some of these Mega-Church's preachers hide behind religion and don't pay taxes. But you the congregation pay all this money into this institution which I call a plantation of slavery. And you must pay your fair share of taxes. Don't get mad! Get even! I don't believe in playing with God! So, I suggest you start a business that there is a need for your product. Remember there is a gift in you, and if I was you, I would try and figure out what is my gift that God gave me to give to this world? Now step out on faith with God speed. Amen! There is much more I could say about the Church, but it has nothing to do with this book. I'm going to write about religion and the Church and how so many people are being deceive and mislead. This book is called the False Prophet of End Time.

THE UNION...

YOUR JOB PROTECTION

I believe that every Plantation (company) needs a union, because your employer (master, boss, supervisor, manager) can terminate your position on your job with no reason for your dismissal. There is a law on the books here in Tennessee. The reason I know that this law exist, is I tried to sue Memphis scrap metal and found out that the employer can terminate you without cause. I could not believe this. If the master doesn't like the way you look or how you smell he or she can fire you and say that you were not qualified for the position that you were hired for. Jake the snake and this other crook from Columbus MS. Made up all kinds of lies about me, so that it appeared that I was incompetent of doing my job. I file a lawsuit about a safety issue. The trucks were not in compliant with the Department of Transportation Safety rules. I believe that they hired illegal aliens, so I called the immigrations people, and nothing was ever done. Why you ask? Because they got enough money to fight off or hire the lawyers to defend them in court. My case never made it to court, because I didn't have money to fight back. That's why I'm so grateful that the Kroger plantation has a union for their truck drivers. They just can't terminate me without cause. But let me say this, if you bring a gun on company property or get caught with drugs in your system or have too many accidents the union can't save your job. You might as well, kiss the baby…. You fired yourself. There's only so much that the union can do. My suggestion to you is, you should try to find a job that has a union, so that you may have some job security. And just maybe your plantation has a pension for your retirement. But always remember that no job is one hundred percent secure. The only job that is one hundred percent secure and you can never be fired is the one job that you create. You start your

very own business. You will not fire, yourself will you?......lol

PROBLEMS WITH MONEY...

IS IT (MONEY) THE ANSWER TO YOUR PROBLEMS?

Ecclesiastes 10:19 *"A feast is made for laughter, and wine maketh merry: but money answereth all things,"*

Johnny Taylor the blues singer says in a song "If you got money, you still got problems. Go to the psychiatrist try to solve them. Hey anyway you look at it, it's still called the blues". The R&B group the O-Jays has a song "for the Love of Money". Is money the answer to your problems? I don't think so, because money can't buy you happiness. I see billionaires and millionaires commit suicide all the time and they got all the money in the world and they are still unhappy. Why?...... For the lack of money can cause a wife to leave her husband for another man who got money, but that doesn't mean that she will be happy. The grass is not always greener on the other side. The bible verse at the beginning of this chapter says that money answers all things. What people fail to realize is that you can't throw money at an emotion or an attitude or if someone says that they don't love you anymore. Money can't buy love! You can buy some happy feelings and some sex, but you can't buy love. If someone is with you, because you got money, they won't be there long, because when the money runs out, and it will! You get the picture! Blues singer Bobby Womack says in a song "Nobody wants you, when you're down and out". When you're broke nobody wants to be your friend. But hit the lottery, and you will have more friends than you can count. It's amazing what money does to some people. I'm broke as I'm writing this book, but I find Joy in the fact that I woke up this morning in my right mind, I got a good job making money to pay my bills. I got clothes on my back and a roof over my head. My wife she might leave, because I'm not making enough money, but we made a covenant with God that we would love each other in sickness and health. For richer or poorer until death do us apart. So if she leaves me, I'm going to let go and let God handle her. But I can see it now, this book becomes a number one seller, and here she comes. But I will deal with that when that happens. Let me say this. All I ever wanted in life is to have enough money to do as I please. What do you mean Zulu? If I wanted to fly to Europe, call the travel agency. It's done! If I need a new car, go buy one. If I need some new clothes, go buy some. If my family is hungry, I got money to feed my family. To me money is a tool? They say that Love makes the world go around, but money greases the wheel. My child needs some new shoes, my wife needs a new dress, I'm working on two jobs trying to do my best. Hey, any way you look at it, I'm still catching the blues.

THE CONCLUSION...

This is where I give my conclusion or my closing arguments about this book Occupational Slavery. The inequality and social economic differences of people is so profound that it is causing a world wide war of a movement that this world has never seen before. The monetary gap between the rich and the poor is getting wider and wider, while the poor people are starving, while trying to live on a plantation wage. So we have come to the end of the rainbow and there is no pot of gold. Like all good things in life, there is a beginning and a ending. So we have come to the end of my book. I sincerely hope and pray that I have inspired and informed you the reader about this system of capitalism which I call Occupational Slavery. I pray that this book gives you the motivation and the inspiration to get up and change your life style. You don't have to be a slave of the system (SOTS). There is hope for you to become a member of the ten percent club. All you have to do is follow the instructions that I have given you in this book. Remember that it will not be easy. And It will not happen over night. It's going to take some time, so be patient and stay focused on your goals. If it was easy, everybody would be doing it. If you really want to change your situation, you must sacrifice your life style. This is what you must do? First things first, set a time line of five or ten years, or maybe three years. Or whatever is best for you and your situation. Then you must change yourself into someone else, who you asked? Mr. Scrooge, the cheap uncle or aunt, EL Cheap-O, or the Stingy Miser!........lol You got to learn how to save your money, especially when you know that the system is design to keep you broke and dependent on your job. Let me show you how to achieve your dreams. Check this out? Let's say that you smoke, Please stop right now! You can do it! Philippians 4: 13 *"I can do all things through Christ, who strengthens me"*. Let's take a closer look at what I'm talking about. Do this even if you don't smoke. If you smoke a pack of cigarettes a day for one year at seven dollars per pack you spend? $2,555.....per year. Look at how much money you could save in one year. If you drink liquor in the amount of one hundred dollars a month for one year, that's $1,200 dollars. If you smoke marijuana everyday at the cost of ten dollars per day....that's $3,650. And if you're a man, you probably got this bill called the pussycat bill.....lol at one hundred dollars a week at fifty-two weeks $5,200.....per year. Let's add this all up. Cigarettes $2,555. Liquor $1,200 Marijuana $3,650 if you're a man Pussycat $5,200 TOTAL....$12,605 dollars you could save every year. Now you do the math in ten short years you could have One Hundred and Twenty-Six Thousand and fifty dollars in your bank account drawing interest. With good credit (something that I have not talked about yet) and the right business plan you can start your own plantation... Now that you have mastered the systems of slavery, (by studying, reading and following the instructions that are in this book) and you know what the master of the plantation is doing to you, to keep you as his slave, you can now free yourself and break the chains of bondage........Now let's talk about credit........ I look at credit like it's a double edge sword or two sided glove. It's good on one hand and it's bad on the other hand. Credit can be a good thing if you know how to use it wisely. But most people don't know how or when to used their credit. You need to learn how to master the game and this system of slavery first. That's why I did not have a chapter on Credit. Credit should be used for emergency only. There are many credit repair businesses that will help you get your credit in good standing, but that's no good if you don't know what the master is doing to you, too keep you broke and in debt. Your credit score should be in the range of 700-850. You should use your credit to buy a house or buy a new car. Do not use your credit cards for any of these National Holidays (Holidays). You should never use your credit cards to buy christmas gifts or buy anything on the major holidays. Zulu's rule # 1. If you can't pay cash for it, don't buy it! Now stick to your game plan and stay focused. I believe in you! The End. Two percent of all book sales go to my non-profit Foundation Please help me support the Good Shepherds Foundation.

Thank You. James Zulu Miller (the Good Shepherd).
Paypal.com/us/fundraiser/charity/3705198

LIST of NATIONAL DAYS

www.lists.org

The following pages are a list of Stupid National Days that are set up to keep you spending your money everyday of the year. Don't fall for the hype!

❋ ❋ ❋

JANUARY 1 New Years Day- National Hangover Day. 2 National personal trainer awareness day. 3 National drinking straw day. 4 National trivia day. 5 National whipped cream day. 6 National technology day. 7 National bobblehead day. 8 National argyle day. 9 National apricot day. 10 National cut your energy costs day. 11 National milk day. 12 National marzipan day. 13 National sticker day. 14 National dress up your pet day. 15 National hat day. 16 National nothing day. 17 National hot buttered rum day. 18 National winnie the pooh day. 19 National popcorn day. 20 National cheese lover's day.

21 National hugging day. 22 National blonde brownie day. 23 National handwriting day. 24 Beer can appreciation day. 25 National opposite day. 26 National spouses day. 27 Do for your country day. 28 National kazoo day. 29 National puzzle day. 30 National croissant day. 31 National inspire your heart with art day.

❊ ❊ ❊

FEBRUARY 1 National freedom day. 2 National groundhog day. 3 Day the music died day. Carrot cake day. 4 Homemade soup day. 5 Shower with a friend day. 6 Frozen yogurt day. 7 Send a card to a friend day. 8 Kite flying day. 9 National Pizza day. 10 National umbrella day. 11 National inventor's day. 12 Plum pudding day. 13 National tortellini day. 14 Valentines day. 15 Singles awareness day. 16 National almond day. 17 National random acts of kindness day. 18 National drink wine day. 19 National chocolate mint day. 20 National love your pet day. 21 National sticky bun day. 22 National margarita day. 23

National toast day. 24 National tortilla chip day. 25 Chocolate covered nut day. 26 Tell a fairy tale day. 27 National strawberry dat. 28 national floral design day. 29 Leap day.

* * *

MARCH 1 National dadgum that's good day. 2 National old stuff day. 3 I want you to be happy day. 4 National grammar day. 5 National cheese doodle day. 6 National oreo cookie day. 7 National cereal day. 8 Womens day, peanut cluster day. 9 National panic day. 10 National mario day. 11National promposal day. 12 National girl scout day. 13 K9 veterans day. 14 National potato chip day. 15 Shoe the world day. 16 Everything you do is right day. 17 ST. Patrick's day. 18 National sloppy joe day. 19 National certified nurses day. 20 National ravioli day. 21 National single parent day. 22 National goof off day. 23 National chip and dip day. 24 National chocolate covered raisin day. 25 National waffle day. 26 National spinach day. 27 Spanish paella day. 28 Something on a stick day. 29 National mom and pop business owners day. 30 National take a walk in the park day. 31 National crayon day.

* * *

APRIL 1 April fool's day. 2 National ferret day. 3 National tweed day. 4 National vitamin c day. 5 National go for broke day. 6 National caramel popcorn day. 7 National beer day. 8 National zoo lovers day. 9 National name yourself day. 10 National siblings day. 11 National pet day. 12 National grilled cheese sandwich day. 13 National scrabble day. 14 National reach as high as you can day. 15 National tax day. 16 National bean counter day. 17 National nothing like a dame day. 18 National animal crackers day. 19 National garlic day. 20 National look alike day. 21 National kindergarten day. 22 National earth day. 23 National talk like shakespeare day. 24 National pigs in a blanket day. 25 National telephone day. 26 National kids and pets day. 27 National tell a story day. 28 National superhero day. 29 National zipper day. 30 National adopt a shelter pet day.

* * *

MAY 1 National Mother goose day. 2 National truffle day. 3 World Press Freedom day. 4 National star wars day. 5 Cinco De Mayo. 6 National nurses day. 7National homebrew day. 8 National have a coke day. 9 National lost sock memorial day. 10 National clean up your room day. 11 National foam rolling day. 12 National odometer day. 13 National apple pie day. 14 National dance like a chicken day. 15 National chocolate chip day. 16 National piercing day. 17 International minecraft day. 18 National visit your relatives day. 19 National devil's food cake day. 20 National pick strawberries day. 21 National memo day. 22 National buy a musical instrument day. 23 National lucky penny day. 24 Nationaal tiara day. 25 National wine day. 26 National blueberry cheesecake day. 27 National cellophane tape day. 28 National hamburger day. 29 National paperclip day. 30 National water a flower day. 31 National macaroon day.

* * *

JUNE 1 Go barefoot day. 2 National rocky road day. 3 Insect repellant awareness day. 4 National hug your cat day. 5 National gingerbread day. 6 National eyewear day. 7 National chocolate ice cream day. 8 National best friends day. 9 Wine and dine day. 10 National iced tea day. 11 National making life beautiful day. 12 National children's day. 13 National sewing machine day. 14 National flag day. 15 Nature photography day. 16 National fudge day. 17 National eat your vegetables day. 18 National go fishing day. 19 National martini day. 20 National ice cream soda day. 21. Go skateboarding day. 22 National chocolate eclair day. 23National hydration day. 24 National pralines day. 25 National strawberry parfait day. 26 National beautician's day. 27 National sunglasses day. 28 National Paul Bunyan day. 29 National camera day. 30National meteor watch day.

✳ ✳ ✳

JULY 1 National postal worker day. 2 National anisette day. 3 National eat your beans day. 4 INDEPENDENCE DAY (July4). 5 National bikini day. 6 National fried chicken day. 7 National strawberry sundae day. 8 National chocolate with almonds day. 9 National sugar cookie day. 10 National pina colada day. 11 National cheer up the lonely day. 12 Eat your jello day. 13 National french fry day. 14 National Nude day. 15 National I love horses day. 16 National corn fritters day. 17 World Emoji day. 18 National sour candy day. 19 National daiquiri day. 20 National lollipop day. 21 National junk food day. 22. National hammock day. 23 National vanilla ice cream day. 24 National drive-thru day. 25 National hot fudge sundae day. 26 National aunt and uncle's day. 27 National creme brulee day. 28 National milk chocolate day. 29 National lasagna day. 30 National cheesecake day. 31 National mutt day.

* * *

AUGUST 1 National raspberry cream pie day. 2 National ice cream sandwich day. 3 National watermelon day. 4 National chocolate chip cookie day. 5 National underwear day. 6 National root beer float day. 7 Purple heart day. 8 National Happiness happens day. 9 Book lover's day. 10 Lazy day. 11 Presidential joke day. 12 National vinyl record day. 13 Internationaal left-handers day. 14 National creamsicle day. 15 National relaxation day. 16 National tell a joke day. 17 National thrift shop day. 18 National bad poetry day. 19 National aviation day. 20 National radio day. 21National senior citizens day. 22 National tooth fairy day. 23 National sponge cake day. 24 National hug your boss day. 25 National banana split day. 26 National dog day. 27 National just because day. 28 National cherry turnovers day. 29 National chop suey day. 30 National toasted marshmallow day. 31 National trail mix day.

❈ ❈ ❈

SEPTEMBER 1 Labor day, National no rhyme (no reason) day. 2 National blueberry popsicle day. 3 U.S. bowling league day. 4 National wildlife day. 5 National cheese pizza day. 6 National read a book day. 7 National beer lover's day. 8 National ampersand day. 9 National teddy bear day. 10 National swap ideas day. 11 NATIONAL DAY OF SERVICE AND REMEMBRANCE. 12 National video games day. 13 National kids take over the kitchen day. 14 National eat a hoagie day. 15 Greenpeace day. 16 National play-doh day. 17 CONSTITUTION DAY AND CITIZENSHIP DAY. 18 Air Force Birthday. 19 Talk like a pirate day. 20 National punch day. 21 National pecan cookie day. 22 American business women's day. 23 National Great American Pot Pie day. 24 National punctuation day. 25 National comic book day. 26 National Good Neighbor day. 27 Nationalchocolate milk day. 28 National strawberry cream pie day. 29 VFW DAY. 30 National chewing gum day. Filipino American History Month Columbus Day (second Monday)

* * *

OCTOBER 1 National homemade cookies day. 2 Custodial workers recognition day. 3 National techies day. 4 National golf day. 5 National do something nice day. 6 National German-American day. 7 National LED light day. 8 National Touch Tag Day. 9 National Chess day. 10 National Holiday Day. 11 National Sausage Pizza Day. 12 National Farmer's Day. 13 Navy Birthday. 14 Be Bald and Be Free Day. 15 National I love lucy day. 16 Dictionary day. 17 National mulligan day. 18 National chocolate cupcake day. 19 National seafood bisque day. 20 National suspenders day. 21 National reptile awareness day. 22 National color day. 23 Nationalboston cream pie day. 24 UNITED NATIONS DAY. 25 National greasy food day. 26 Day of the Deployed. 27 Navy Day. 28 National chocolate day. 29 National cat day. 30 National candy corn day. 31 HALLOWEEN.

❊ ❊ ❊

Thanksgiving day (fourth Thursday of November).. **NOVEMBER** 1 National brush day. 2 National deviled egg day. 3 National housewife's day. 4 National use your common sense day. 5 National love your red hair day. 6 National nachos day. 7 National hug a bear day. 8 National x-ray day. 9 WORLD FREEDOM DAY. 10 MARINE CORPS BIRTHDAY 11 VETERANS DAY. 12 National fancy rat and mouse day. 13 World Kindness day. 14 National spicy guacamole day. 15 National clean out your refrigerator day. 16 National button day. 17 National Baklava day. 18 National occult day. 19 National play monopoly day. 20 National peanut butter fudge day. 21 National stuffing day. 22 National cranberry relish day. 23 National cashew day. 24 National sardines day. 25 National parfait day. 26 National cake day. 27 National pins & needles day. 28 National french toast day. 29 Electronic Greetings day. 30 National mousse day.

* * *

DECEMBER 1 National bartender appreciation day. 2 National mutt day. 3 National roof over your head day. 4 National dice day. 5 National bathtub party day. 6 National microwaveoven day. 7 National Pearl Harbor Remembrance day. 8 Pretend to be a time traveler day. 9 Bike shop day, National pastry day. 10 Nobel Prize day. 11 International Mountain day. 12 National ding-a-ling day. 13 National cocoa day. 14 National bouillabaisse day. 15 National wear your pearls day. 16 National chocolate covered anything day. 17 Wright Brothers day. 18 Nationals bake cookies day. 19 National hard candy day. 20 National sangria day. 21 Crossword puzzle day. 22 National Date nut bread day. 23 National roots day. 24 CHRISTMAS EVE. 25 CHRISTMAS. 26 KWANZAA. 27 National fruitcake day. 28 Pledge of Allegiance day. 29 Tick Tock day. 30 Bacon day. 31 National Champagne day.